# An Introduction
# to Sports Acrobatics

# Morgan Smith

# An Introduction to Sports Acrobatics

**Stanley Paul**
London Melbourne Sydney Auckland Johannesburg

*To Dr Victor Paul Wierville, President and Founder of 'The Way International', to my wife Sharon and to my sons Brett, Darren, Steve, Scott and Ted*

Stanley Paul & Co. Ltd

An imprint of the Hutchinson Publishing Group

17–21 Conway Street, London W1P 6JD

Hutchinson Group (Australia) Pty Ltd
30–32 Cremorne Street, Richmond South, Victoria 3121
PO Box 151, Broadway, New South Wales 2007

Hutchinson Group (NZ) Ltd
32–34 View Road, PO Box 40–086, Glenfield, Auckland 10

Hutchinson Group (SA) (Pty) Ltd
PO Box 337, Bergvlei 2012, South Africa

First published 1982
© Morgan Smith 1982

Set in Linotron Plantin by Willmer Brothers Ltd.

Printed in Great Britain by The Anchor Press Ltd
and bound by Wm Brendon & Son Ltd
both of Tiptree, Essex

ISBN 0 09 146230 4 (cased)
       0 09 146231 2 (paper)

# Contents

# Acknowledgements

I welcome this opportunity to thank several people who were instrumental in bringing me to the point of writing this book: Dick Gradley, whose faithfulness to coaching and sincerity gave me the firm foundation upon which to build my career; the British Amateur Gymnastics Association, especially John Atkinson, for foreseeing the tremendous future in sports acrobatics; and Nik Stuart MBE, whose humour, wit and wisdom motivated me to think big and attain my goals.

Also a sincere thank you to the following people for their help in the preparation of this book: Larry Molloy, New York, USA, an Acro technician whose attention to detail leaves absolutely nothing to be desired; Bob Johnson, New Orleans, USA, my photographer whose patience and skill resulted in the excellent pictures found in this book; and Sharon Smith, New Orleans, USA, my wife and personal editor who took my many pages of notes, made them readable and typed my manuscript.

# Foreword

My first meeting with Morgan Smith was at Gotts Park School some fifteen years ago in the city of Leeds, Yorkshire. I could tell that, even at that early age, he had been bitten by the 'Acro' bug, because of his unusual adaptation of the cricket nets – they were held out and used for practising double back somersaults.

From those early days to the present he has displayed a constant creative ability which, combined with his boundless energy, has enabled him to make contributions to the sport throughout the world from the freezing snows of the USSR to the vitalizing sun of California.

Morgan Smith was the first western acrobat to bring medals back through the Iron Curtain and the first Briton to perform the 'full in back out' on the floor. Within two years of starting his own school in America his gymnasts were selected to represent the USA at the World Acrobatic Championships in Europe. He has a fine appreciation of the technicalities of the sport and, like all true coaches, understands the value of the basic elements. Luckily he has found the time to commit this to paper.

So *An Introduction to Sports Acrobatics* is a book for carrying in your training bag. It occupies a place of honour on my desk as an ever present reference for all who enter the exciting field of sports acrobatics.

Nik Stuart MBE
*Director of Technical Development*
*British Amateur Gymnastics Association*

# Introduction

Within the heart of every man, woman and child lies a desire to turn a somersault. We watch with envy the ease with which the astronaut effortlessly turns within the pressureless training capsule. There is an undeniable wish to be in his shoes as he defies all the laws of gravity. Today's astronaut may not realize it, but he is demonstrating a sport which has been in existence for thousands of years. The word acrobat is derived from the Greek word 'acrobatos', meaning to climb or to rise, and acrobatics is often referred to as the 'mother of all sports', particularly in Eastern Europe. From ancient art we can tell that it was performed long ago by the Chinese, Egyptians, Greeks and Romans and has been kept alive through the ages by circus acrobats and others.

It was officially recognized as a sport in 1973 when the International Federation of Sports Acrobatics was formed, and is defined as a branch of gymnastics in which the exercises are performed in pairs or groups of three or four. The first World Championships held under IFSA sanctions were in Moscow in 1974 and now take place every other year, alternating with the World Cup competition.

Basically, this book serves two main purposes. First, it is an instructional book for beginners, both gymnasts and coaches/teachers including sports acrobatics on the curriculum for the first time. Secondly, it sets out a junior competitive programme for schools, clubs and universities. One need not be concerned with the competitive programme in the beginning, but, as the interest and level of skill increases, so does the desire to compete. Providing the progressions are followed according to this text, beginners should find no difficulty in attaining the level required for the junior competitive programme. The chapter setting this out also details the rules and gives advice on what the judges are looking for in competition.

Sports acrobatics is a wonderful sport of movement and body control and this book will give everyone the opportunity to experience the many thrills of gymnastics either through participation or coaching.

# 1 Safety and Health

## Safety

Get your programme off to a good start by creating a healthy, safe and pleasant environment in which to enjoy learning sports acrobatics.

Safety is an essential part of any sport, particularly for beginners. All of the safety guidelines which apply to sport in general should always be followed in sports acrobatics:

1 Do not chew gum
2 Do not wear jewellery
3 Report all injuries to the instructor in charge
4 Make sure there is a Red Cross first aid kit in the gym and everyone knows where it is
5 For injuries use I – ice
                      C – compression
                      E – elevation
6 Emergency numbers should be kept by the nearest phone
7 Never move an athlete with a suspected neck or spine injury
8 Check for proper breathing, control bleeding and treat for shock
9 Red Cross first aid procedures should be used whenever possible. Remember, the athlete usually has a good idea of the seriousness of his injury by the pain he feels
10 If in the slightest doubt call an ambulance or doctor

In addition there are elements of safety which are more specific to sports acrobatics:

1 Be aware of limitations
2 Do not attempt skills for which you are unprepared – use progressions
3 Participants should assist one another, especially when height and rotation are involved, but only when the correct standing-in or spotting techniques are understood
   Spotting is a term used to describe support given to a performer by some external source, either to give additional momentum or to guard against falls. Hence partners or persons standing by to help are called spotters, and a safety belt fastened to the roof to support a performer in flight or when out of reach of partner assistance is called a spotting belt or rig (see figure 90, page 56)
4 Make full use of spotting belts and landing mats

These precautions can be summed up in the *Acrobatic Code of Safety*:

*A*wareness: be aware of the activities going on around you
*C*apability: know the capabilities of yourself and your partners
*R*esponsibility: be responsible for the welfare of your partners
*O*rganization: an organized workout is always safe and more productive

## Health

Unlike most sports, sports acrobatics participants work in close proximity with other people. Therefore some fundamental rules of hygiene should be meticulously observed:

1 Feet should be clean
2 Fingernails and toenails should be trimmed and clean
3 Hair should be tied back
4 Be clean, clean, clean

## Clothing

Proper clothing is important in all sporting activities and sports acrobatics is no exception. It is recommended that the clothing listed below be worn for workouts (but note that bare feet are permissible if preferred):

Boys: T-shirts, shorts, socks and soft gym shoes
Girls: leotard, socks and soft gym shoes

# 2 The Warm-Up

'I don't need to do a warm-up.'
  'Warm-ups are boring.'
  'I don't want to waste my energy.'

Statements like these are heard in every sport and usually come from the inexperienced. A warm-up should be beneficial and, like warming up a car, should get the oil moving in the parts. It should be the first thing one does after changing into workout clothes. A correctly choreographed warm-up should inspire the most apathetic gymnast and create a feeling of well-being and confidence. It should also be interesting and fun. This is the time to use all of the body, to encourage mobility and flexibility.

As with any physical activity, preparation is of paramount importance, providing both a physical and mental stimulus. The warm-up in sports acrobatics must awaken the zest for maximum effort in the workout and should be continuous, without long pauses. Ideally it should peak just before the end and the adrenalin should be flowing.

Length and format of the warm-up should be adjusted according to the mood of the class. Sports acrobatics requires a lot more attention to the individual than do most team sports. The warm-up, for individual or class, should last about twenty minutes.

The ideal class size per coach is twelve to fifteen students. The coach should call the students together and, after a brief on the objectives of the lesson, lead the class into the warm-up. Music can energize the most lethargic and a good 4/4 time beat should be introduced as soon as possible.

The same principles apply if it is an individual warming up – be organized!

## Warm-up exercises

The first warm-up exercises stimulate the heart and breathing (the cardiovascular system).

### Exercise 1 Jogging

a Start by doing some light jogging on your toes then run around the gym with your arms hanging loosely by your sides (one or two laps)
b Run one lap while kicking your heels up behind
c Run one lap while kicking your legs up in front

### Exercise 2 Skipping

a Skip sideways around the gym for four counts and then skip in the opposite direction for four counts. Repeat several times

### Exercise 3 Jumping

a With your feet together and arms down by your sides, jump forward and backward and side to side. Act like a penguin!

### Exercise 4 Pirouettes

a Feet together, jump four quarter turns to the right and repeat to the left
b Jump one half turn to the right and then to the left
c Jump a full turn to the right and to the left

Repeat this exercise twice.

The remainder of the warm-up exercises listed deal with stretching the muscles to improve the mobility of various joints. Certain points should always be remembered when practising stretching exercises for mobility:

1 Always ensure the muscles and joints are properly warmed-up before stretching
2 Always use some external force, i.e. partner, coach or gravity, to stretch the muscle a little bit farther than normal
3 Always use slow smooth relaxing pressure, sustained for 20–30 seconds
4 Never use violent stretching movements, these will be ineffective and may result in torn muscles

### Exercise 5 Joint rotations

a Clasp hands together and vigorously rotate them, loosening the wrists
b Roll head from side to side and around in a circle, loosening the neck muscles

### Exercise 6 Torso stretching

a Place feet shoulder width apart and stretch arms vertically above head. Lean over to the left, then to the right. Inhale as you stretch to the side, exhale as you return to the upright position. Keep back straight
b Repeat this exercise with arms stretched sideways

### Exercise 7 Shoulder stretching

a Circle arms forward
b Circle arms backward

### Exercise 8 Hamstring stretching

a Legs apart, bend forward from the waist and allow upper body to hang loosely. The object is to place the chest on the thighs. Twist and turn during this exercise so as to stretch the hamstrings

b Return to upright position and slowly bend backwards. Try to see the wall behind you. Always use steady, relaxing pressure when stretching to avoid muscle tears

### Exercise 9 Shoulder and hamstring stretching

a Legs apart and arms above head, touch the floor in front of your feet. Reach back through the legs as far as you can
b Return to starting position and extend arms back to stretch shoulders

### Exercise 10 Leg and hip stretching

a Place legs wide apart, arms out at sides. Lunge, bending one knee four times; repeat on the other knee
b Straddle to maximum stretch and, using your hands as support on the floor, walk forward and backward
c Sit with legs wide apart. Extend your arms above your head and stretch forward to place chest on first one knee, then the other. Hold the stretch position for a minimum of 4 seconds each time
d Sit with legs together straight out in front of you. Stretch toes to a point and then back towards the body. Repeat this several times to loosen ankles and feet
e Sit with legs together in front of you and arms extended above your head. Lean forward to place chest on knees. Repeat four times
f Sit with legs together straight out in front of you. Roll backwards and touch the floor behind you with your toes, keeping legs straight. Roll forwards and straddle legs to place chest on the floor. Repeat four times
g Sit with legs together in front of you and reach behind as far as you can. Bend your knees up and move seat away from hands. When you have reached your limit, swing your knees to the left and right

h Return to sitting position with one leg bent and one straight. Swing the straight leg up left and right of the face, keeping seat on the floor. Repeat with the other leg

*Exercise 11 Stomach and thigh stretching*

a Kneel and sit back on stretched-out toes. Place hands behind you on the floor and stretch back as far as possible at the same time pushing the hips forward

b A useful exercise for *strengthening* stomach and thighs is as follows: kneel upright with toes stretched out behind you and hands on hips. Keeping straight from head to knees, lean backwards as far as possible without loosing balance and then pull back to the upright position.

*Exercise 12 Spine and shoulder flexibility*

a Lie on your back and push up to a backbend. Repeat four times (figure 1)

Figure 1

# 3 Tumbling

Besides being a sport on its own, tumbling is the descriptive name for a series of agility skills performed in sequence along a special strip of mats (usually 30 metres long). Recently the introduction of the 'ski runs' has brought a new dimension to tumbling, allowing triple somersaults and safe development of very high jumps. These are so called because the original runs were made by laying old overland skis side by side across timber battens and then covering them with mats. This, however, is very expensive and modern ski runs are constructed from special spring panels 6–8 feet in length.

Basic tumbling skills should be thoroughly perfected before moving on to higher risk elements. I am constantly amazed at how many experienced tumblers find some fundamental skills difficult. So practise these.

The class should line up in two columns to reduce waiting time and utilize the tumbling mats more efficiently (figure 2). This will help to make even basic rolls challenging and interesting for the beginner and experienced tumbler alike. Note that the term 'chassé' is derived from the French word meaning 'to chase'. In gymnastics and dance the term simply means to skip forward, backward and sideways, with the rear foot 'chasing' the first. Chassé steps before and after tumbling elements such as cartwheels encourage the gymnast to maintain good technique as well as to develop a sense of rhythm.

Practise agilities in the following sequence:

Forward rolls
Handstand forward rolls
Variety of forward rolls with tuck, pike, straddle, etc.

Backward rolls
Backward rolls to handstand (extension roll)
Variety of backward rolls with tuck, pike, straddle, etc.

Cartwheels
Cartwheel, chassé, cartwheel
Round-off
Round-off, jump half turn, cartwheel

Forward walkovers
Front handsprings
Front handspring walkout

Backward walkovers
Back handsprings (from standing, with spotters)
Round-off back handspring

Combinations of all the above

The rest of this chapter gives specific instructions for teaching and performing the tumbling skills listed above. These must be mastered before progressing to the acrobatic pair exercises.

Figure 2 ▶

## Forward roll (figure 3)

Begin by standing upright, feet together, arms by your side. Raise your arms so they are horizontal with the floor. Bend your knees to the squat position. Place both hands on the mat and tuck your head down. Push off with both feet and roll over onto the back of your shoulders, keeping knees firmly in a tight tuck position. As feet make contact with the mat, extend your hands forward so that body weight falls over your knees, and stand up boldly.

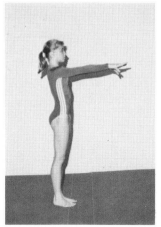

Figure 3

## Handstand forward roll (figure 4)

The prerequisite for this skill is a positive kick to handstand.

Stand with your arms extended above your head, body taut, stomach held in. Lift one leg off the ground, extend forward and kick to handstand. Allow the handstand to fall slightly forward and then slowly bend your arms while tucking your head between them. As with the basic forward roll, maintain the tuck position until weight is over your knees. Then stand boldly.

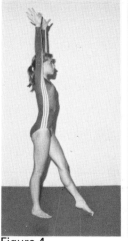

Figure 4

## Backward roll (figure 5 right to left)

Begin with your arms extended above your head. Bend your knees to a squat position, keeping your eyes trained on your knees. Allow weight to fall backwards and slowly roll onto your back. Keeping chin on chest, place the palms of your hands (turned inwards) on the mat behind your head. As seat and hips pass over the vertical point, a strong thrust of the arms will ensure a final standing position.

Figure 5

Figure 6

Figure 7

*Point to note:* the incline method is a useful aid for the beginner learning forward and backward rolls. This entails placing tumbling mats upon benches which have been raised at one end. This set-up helps familiarize the young gymnast with forward and backward motion.

## Cartwheel (figure 6)

Begin with your arms extended above your head. Press your arms against your ears to ensure maximum stretch. Lift the right leg (start with the left leg if preferred) parallel to the floor and look down to the extended toes. Allow this leg to step to the floor immediately following with both arms. Keep stomach tight, back straight and maintain legs and arms in extended form. The initial momentum is helped by stepping sideways on the extended leading leg and following through with arms and head. Always aim to finish the cartwheel with arms extended above your head so that you will have no difficulty in continuing with another element of tumbling. Remember to practise the cartwheel in both directions, left and right.

*Variations*

Side chassé, step, cartwheel. Repeat
Run two or three steps, cartwheel

## Round-off

This is the most underestimated skill I know.
So many times I have been asked to check a
student's back handspring or back flip after
the coach has said that he is astonished at the
inconsistencies of the performance. The
same coach is horrified when I draw his
attention to the fact that the round-off is
incorrect and consequently the back handspring or any skill that follows is not getting a
fair start.

A round-off is not the world's easiest skill!
The transition from forward motion through
a 180° turn to finish facing in the opposite
direction is difficult to achieve. A round-off
is the only skill at this level of agility that
converts forward into backward motion
(figure 7).

*Points to note:*
1 The 'snap down' motion is essential to the
   round-off (figure 8). The initial thrust is
   created by bending the legs at the knees. A
   sharp straightening action of the legs
   followed by a strong push through the
   shoulders and hands will produce suf-
   ficient vigour to land you in a standing
   position
2 Ensure that you have mastered the
   cartwheel from a running step. Bring your
   legs together at the top of the cartwheel
   and with a twist of the hips, snap legs
   down to the floor. Aim to place the feet at
   approximately an arm's length away from
   the hands
3 Turn second hand in direction of the turn
   (figure 9)

Figure 8

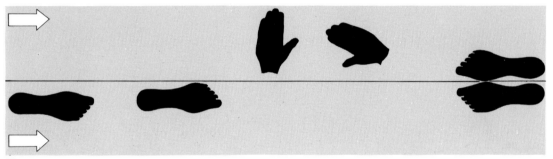

Figure 9

Figure 10

4 Reach forward away from the take-off leg to obtain maximum benefit from the hurdle step (described on page 24)

## Variations

Round-off, jump 180° turn, cartwheel
Cartwheel, chassé, round-off
Cartwheel, chassé, round-off, 180° turn, cartwheel

## Forward walkover

Most beginners find this relatively easy, providing enough time has been spent on the prerequisites – handstand, backbend, flexibility.

Begin with a complete extension of the body, arms above head, take-off leg stretched out in front. Lunge forward and place hands on floor. Try to achieve maximum extension at all times. Make a strong, positive kick to handstand, remembering to keep legs in the split position from take-off. The leading leg should touch the floor before you push off with your hands (figure 10).

With a hand spot in the small of the back and under the shoulders, it is possible to achieve positive results in a very short time. (The spotting technique is described on page 11. A coach or partner assisting provides a hand spot.)

*Points to note:*
1 Hands should be approximately 6 inches apart
2 There should be no angle between the arms and trunk on take-off; the body, shoulders and arms should be in a straight line. Likewise, on landing, when the leading foot contacts the floor there should be no angle at the hips
3 Arms remain pressed against head to maintain rigid form and avoid the head making an angle with the body
4 Do not be tempted to lift hands from floor too soon

## Front handspring

This is one of the most challenging of all tumbling elements. A technically perfect handspring requires a lot of practice and

understanding. The obvious prerequisite is the positive kick to handstand which can be practised by kicking up to handstand against a wall or with the assistance of a partner.

You must become familiar with the *hurdle step* which forms the beginning of the skill. A lot of attention must be paid to this as it must be perfected if you are to achieve a good front handspring. I realize that running or hopping around the gym is not the most exciting exercise in the world, but a little consideration here will save hours of frustration later. Problems should be isolated and worked on as early as possible.

Start by taking two or three steps and hop on one foot while lifting the opposite leg up in front of you. At this stage the leg may be straight or bent depending upon the individual.

## Primary flight method (figure 11)

The coach takes a confident stand approximately three steps in front of the gymnast

who should feel through the shoulders the push that is achieved from the thrust of the hands.

*Points to note:*
1 Arms must not bend
2 Hands should face forwards

Figure 11

3 Maximum extension should be maintained, particularly at the point of take-off
4 Shoulders must not protrude farther than the hands

*Platform method* (figure 12 right to left)

When the previous progressions have been mastered, the complete movement can be attempted with the aid of a platform (which can be made from benches) covered with a mat, and a landing mat. The next stage is to perform the same skill on a regular mat surface.

## Front handspring walkout (figure 13)

The walkout is really a continuation of the handspring and therefore a good, consistent handspring must be achieved before attempting this skill. The only difference between the two is that with the handspring walkout the legs do not come together at the top of the handstand.

*Points to note:*
1 Do not try to keep legs too far apart. Begin with only splitting legs a little and gradually work up to a good split-leg position
2 The head should be in a natural position. Do not force the head forward as this will increase speed of landing which may result in a fall
3 Both legs must be straight. This is especially important for the leading leg as it guarantees that a straight line is maintained from top to toe

### Variations

Handspring walkout, cartwheel, chassé, round-off
Handspring walkout, handspring

## Backward walkover

The prerequisites for this skill are a good handstand and backbend.

◀ Figure 12

Stand with arms extended upwards, firmly pressing against the head. Turn hands inward. Lift one leg parallel to the floor and bend slowly and confidently backwards, looking at your hands. Head, arms and chest should move as one.

When the hands make contact with the floor, push off with the supporting foot, all the time maintaining the flowing motion as the body passes through a positive handstand to finish (figure 14). You should finish standing vertically with arms still raised above the head.

## Variations

Backward walkover continued to splits
Backward walkover, turn, cartwheel

Figure 13

Figure 14

## Back handspring (back flip or flik flak)

I don't know of any element in tumbling that has as many coaching variations as the back handspring, and a good coach should become familiar with as many different techniques as possible.

The method I describe is the Russian one which, in my experience, is the most successful.

The back handspring is primarily used to build up speed and momentum as a take-off

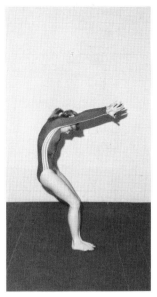

Figure 15

Figure 16

platform for numerous flips. Therefore, as with the round-off, the technique must be as efficient as possible.

Begin by familiarizing yourself with the off-balance position which results from trying to sit in an imaginary chair. Feel the weight on your heels (figure 15). Now proceed with the complete skill, but only with the aid of one or even two spotters (figure 16). Slowly bring your arms down by your sides, bend your knees to a sitting position and with one continuous flowing motion, throw your arms back over your head and stretch backwards over the arms of the spotters. When you feel your hands make contact with the floor continue the movement of your legs through to a snap down as described for the round-off (page 21). Then, with a thrust of the hands and a kick of the legs, you will arrive in an upright, standing position (figure 17 right to left).

*Points to note:*
1 The arms should be as close to the ears as possible. This will ensure correct direction and will also eliminate the possibility of smacking your favourite spotter in the face!
2 Hands should be turned inwards to avoid unnecessary pressure on the wrists on landing. The proper positioning of the hands also assists in producing an efficient snap down
3 Head should not turn sideways. This is a problem if one does not have complete confidence in oneself. Go back to the build-up and regain confidence. *Never practise a fault*
4 Swing both arms together. An off-centre back handspring will result if the arms are out of line with each other
5 Head should be kept down as long as possible. It is not necessary to throw your head back violently to obtain a good back handspring. Excessive throwing back of the head creates an arched back and makes the shoulder, hip and hand alignment wrong

Remember, flips go up and back, handsprings just go back – keep your back handsprings *long*, *low* and *fluent*.

◀ Figure 17

# 4 Pair Exercises

When the class has mastered the tumbling skills, the gymnasts will be ready to move on to acrobatic pair exercises. The best way to start is to line everyone up by height, divide the line in half and match up partners. The idea is to have the larger students as lower and the smaller students as upper partners (figures 18 and 19). If the class is mixed, don't hesitate to pair a strong boy with a smaller girl. They will act as ideal partners to show the rest of the class the correct techniques. However, it is not a good idea to assign partners on a permanent basis at first. A change of partners is often a good incentive to work harder and also helps to avoid personality clashes.

The coach must be sure that all the gymnasts are familiar with the methods and techniques required to enable them to perform the skill comfortably, safely and correctly. One pair should be selected to demonstrate the exercise for the rest of the class and the coach can then point out the progressions of the skill as it is performed.

Work on one skill at a time. In this way the gymnasts can assist one another with spotting and encouragement as progress is made. Utilize the matted area efficiently and

Figure 18

make sure that each pair has enough space in which to work safely and productively.

It is essential for gymnasts to understand that compatibility is the key to a successful partnership. Both the upper and lower partners in the pair have an equally important role. No gymnast should be allowed to assume that his role is the superior one.

## Balance

Balance very simply means a state of equilibrium or equalness in the forces acting on a body so as to keep it stationary or static.

There are many factors which affect balance but the most important for the purposes of sports acrobatics are the number of points of contact the body has and what they are in contact with. The easiest form of balancing is done on the ground, which is immovable and constitutes no variables. Standing on our feet is a simple two-point balance which we take for granted. The wider the legs are apart, the more secure the balance because the effective base is wider. As the legs are brought together, the base becomes smaller and the balance less secure. Lifting one foot off the floor makes the base area smaller still, so balances are even more difficult on one leg.

The headstand has three points of contact with the ground which make an equilateral triangle if a line is drawn joining the position of the hands and forehead (see page 35, figure 31).

The handstand is much more difficult to hold in balance because there are only two points of contact and they are in a line, making a very small thin base. The one-arm handstand is the most difficult of all.

Virtually all areas of the body may be balanced on and, depending on the size of the

Figure 19

effective base produced, are more or less difficult.

In pair work, the lower partner acts as the base for the upper partner, or in the simple pair balances as the support, or as base and support. Figures 21, 22 and 24 show a simple supported handstand. Figures 26, 27, 28 and 29 are examples of the bottom partner acting as base and support. Figure 54 (page 41) shows the lower partner acting as base only.

There is a very distinct difference between balancing on the floor and balancing unsupported with a partner. In the first instance the person performing the balance is responsible for maintaining the balance. However, in the pair balances, it is the responsibility of the lower partner to balance the upper one, who must keep an absolutely fixed body position. When both top and bottom try to keep the balance there is confusion, since neither can anticipate the other.

The ideal top part of a pair should be light and have very good body control and tension.

There are innumerable combinations possible between upper and lower partner, for example:

Feet to thighs
Hands to thighs
Feet to feet
Feet to shoulders
Hands to feet
Hands to hands, etc.

A smooth flowing change from balance to balance mixed with some degree of agility, brings the sport of acrobatics to life.

*Ten basic balance exercises* (figures 20 to 29)

These first ten exercises are used mainly to ensure that the pairs understand the basic principles of balance. (The coach may decide to change the position of certain students according to the ratio of their weight and ability.)

1  Arch and extend in the balance position for three seconds. Relax and repeat (figure 20)
2  Lift up, hold for three seconds, lower (figure 21)
3  From sitting position, extend to horizontal and return to sitting. Hold for three seconds (figure 22)
4  Backbend to grasp knees. Bend and raise one leg into the 'stag' position shown. Extend leg (figure 23)
5  Front support stand. Keeping body rigid, push up five times (figure 24)
6  Straight support stand (figure 25)
7  Bent knee stand (figure 26)
8  Straddle leg stand (figure 27)
9  Arched back stand (figure 28)
10  Stag stand on knees and hands of partner (figure 29)

Figure 20

Figure 21

Figure 22

Figure 23

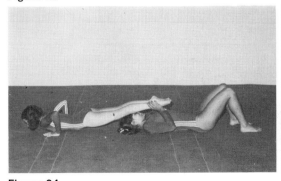 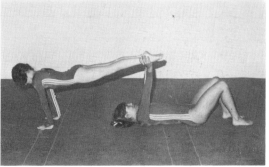

Figure 24

Figure 25

Figure 26

Figure 29

Figure 30

Figure 32

Figure 27

Figure 28

Figure 31

## Intermediate balance exercises

### Headstand

This first, fully inverted balance requires a three-point base of support over which the body is aligned and centred (figures 30, 31 and 32).

*Points to note:*
1 Weight should be distributed equally between arms and head
2 Look at the mat
3 Position the head so that the weight is towards the forehead

Figure 33

Figure 34

Figure 35

Figure 36

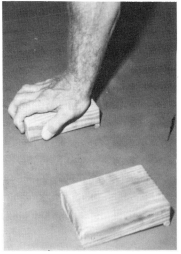
Figure 37

Figure 38

Figure 39

4 Bring the hips up into balance before extending the legs
5 Extend the legs upwards as slowly as possible
6 The final position should be fully extended with all muscles tight, especially stomach, hips, legs and toes

If the headstand is performed properly it will facilitate the learning of the next element, the handstand.

### Supported handstand

The top partner of the pair extends arms above head and steps forward to kick to a straight handstand. The bottom partner assists the balance by grasping his calves. This balance should be maintained for 5 seconds and the top partner returns to a standing position by lowering one leg and then the other (figure 33).

*Points to note:*
1 Hands should point forward, shoulder-width apart. (Girls find the handstand much easier if the hands are less than shoulder-width apart. Ideally, you

should feel the arms touching the side of the head while in balance. Depending on how flexible a boy's shoulders are, this same principle applies)
2 Head should be down between the arms
3 Stomach should be pulled in tight
4 Toes, hips and shoulders in line
5 Toes should be pointed
6 Pelvic muscles should be tense

### Variations

Lunge supported stag handstand (figure 34)
Lunge supported split handstand (figure 35)
Split supported split handstand (figure 36)

### Balancing blocks

These are the oldest, but still the most effective, aids to a better understanding of the art of balance. Simply take a piece of $4 \times 2$ inch wood and cut off two sections, each 6 inches long. You should now have two blocks of wood rather like house bricks. One end of each block should be slightly raised to aid the correct balance position (figures 37, 38 and 39).

Figure 40　　　　　Figure 41

Figure 42　　　　　Figure 43　　　　　Figure 44

### Handstand progressions, low to high

*Handstand on thighs* (figure 40): the top partner kicks up to handstand from behind and to the side of the lower partner who holds top firmly at the waist, arms straight. Top must remain taut and straight. Top may dismount with a forward roll, or a forward walkover with partner's assistance, or cartwheel out to the side.

*Cartwheel mount to handstand on thighs* (figure 41): the partners begin by facing each other. Top stands one step away to the side of lower partner who kneels. Top extends arms above head and cartwheels, placing hands on lower partner's thighs.

The lower partner, assisting direction by placing one hand on top's leading hip, then stabilizes the balance and top brings legs together in handstand.

*Stag handstand on thighs* (figure 42): top partner kicks up from behind and to the side of lower partner. Bottom partner transfers hands from top's waist to position shown. Top dismounts with a forward walkover.

*Handstand on one knee – low* (figure 43): this is a progression from handstand on thighs. The lower partner must assist top with the mount to handstand and must maintain a firm base by turning the supporting foot out. Top can dismount with a forward walkover or a cartwheel to the side.

*Handstand on one knee – high* (figure 44): this is a progression from handstand on one knee (low) and the lower partner especially will find this balance easier to maintain once the previous one is accomplished.

## Shoulder/knee balances, lying

Gymnasts should be encouraged to act as spotters for each other in this and all other pair group activities.

*Points to note:*
1 The bottom partner must give the top partner a firm base on which to balance. Knees and arms must be firm

2 The top partner grasps the bottom partner's legs just above the knees and leans forward to allow the bottom partner to take the weight at the shoulders
3 Once the top partner has kicked up as if to do a handstand with the seat over the centre of gravity, the skill is relatively easy. Top must not take off until the bottom partner has a firm grip of the shoulders (figure 45)
4 Top should keep stomach tight. Once the tuck balance position has been achieved, extend legs up vertically to a straight shoulder/knee balance (figure 46)
5 Bottom partner spreads and raises legs to a 90° angle
6 Top moves legs into a stag position with one knee bent and raised (figure 47)
7 Top dismounts with a forward walkover

## Shoulder/knee balance sequence

The three elements of this balance shown in the photographs (figures 48, 49 and 50) provide an excellent example of correct progression. Practising this short sequence will develop a strong sense of balance in both partners.

Once these three balances have been accomplished, add further skills to start and dismount. A challenging routine will evolve by adding a little choreography and a tumble or two to these basic balances.

## Free shoulder balance (figure 51)

This should not be attempted until the previous shoulder/knee balance has been mastered.

*Points to note:*
1 The top partner transfers one hand at a time, grasping his partner's wrists firmly
2 Top should try to pull his shoulders down into his partner's hands in order to maintain a rigid balance

Figure 45

Figure 46

Figure 47

Figure 48

Figure 49

Figure 50

3 Top's stomach should be tight and body as straight as possible
4 The bottom partner, arms straight at all times, fulfils the role of balancer once top has transferred both hands to his wrists

*Front swan on feet* (figures 52, 53 and 54)

The swan position displays a controlled arched back. The partner who is to perform the swan must practise the position many times to become aware of the body tension required and this can be done on the floor and also with the aid of a box top, wall bars or spotters (figure 52). The partner who is to act as the base must have a clear understanding of feet position – heels together, toes 6 inches apart (see figure 55).

The next step is to perform the skill without any external aids but with hand support (figure 53). The complete skill is a free front swan on feet (figure 54).

Figure 52

Figure 51

Figure 53

*Points to note:*
1 The bottom partner must not release hand support until the balance is felt
2 The bottom partner must keep legs as straight and as vertical as possible
3 Top must maintain a firm, tight swan position at all times
4 The bottom partner must always have heels together and toes 6 inches apart, and should feel pressure on toes and heels while maintaining balance

Figure 54

Figure 55

Figure 56

Figure 57

## Back swan on feet (figures 55, 56 and 57)

*Points to note:*

1 The bottom partner's feet support top in the lower back ensuring that when top is in the back swan position the pivot does not restrict the arch

2 To get into position, top must stand with his back to his partner's feet. Top, turning hands outwards, takes hold of his partner's hands. The bottom partner bends his legs and allows top to backbend into position, straightening legs as the balance is felt

3 The position of the feet is the same as for the front swan – heels together, toes 6 inches apart

## Dismount for back swan

The bottom partner places his hands firmly on top's shoulders and, giving direction with feet and legs, guides top over through a backward walkover.

## Thighstand with hand support (figure 58)

*Points to note:*

1 The bottom partner maintains a firm base by placing feet apart and bending knees to a squat stand

2 The bottom partner takes hold of top's hands and confidently assists him into a standing position on thighs

3 Top must step up vertically to avoid pulling his partner off balance

4 Top must turn feet out to maintain a firm balance

5 The bottom partner must lean backwards to counterbalance top's weight and maintain a stable base

6 Both partners must avoid the tendency to round their backs which should remain straight

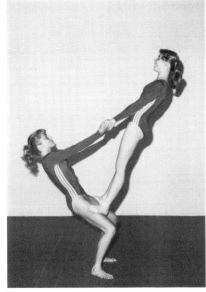

Figure 58

Figure 59

Figure 60        Figure 61

1 The bottom partner transfers one hand at a time from top's hands to the back of upper thighs
2 He must grasp top's thighs firmly and apply downward pressure to stabilize the balance
3 The bottom partner must try to encircle the thighs, making it impossible for a loss of grip to occur

## Thighstand variations

*Facing forward with leg support* (figure 60): the bottom partner, grasping top above hips while top takes hold of his wrists, assists with a vertical lift to thighstand. The bottom partner maintains the balance by applying downward pressure to top's thighs and leaning back to counterbalance.

*Facing forward with hand support* (figure 61): this is a continuation of the previous balance. The bottom partner transfers one hand at a time from top's thighs to hands. Top, remaining straight and rigid throughout,

## Thighstand with leg support (figure 59)

This is a progression from the previous balance and those six points should therefore be repeated and continued as follows.

must always keep feet turned out and maintain pressure on toes and heels during the balance.

### Front scale on one knee, low (figure 62)

A scale is a single leg balance.

*Points to note:*
1 Top steps vertically onto his partner's knees, turning support foot outwards
2 Top moves slowly into a scale position, maintaining balance at all times
3 Both partners must keep arms straight during the balance
4 The bottom partner must turn support foot outwards to help maintain a firm base, and lean back to counterbalance top's weight and position

Figure 62

### Front scale on one knee, high (figure 63)

*Points to note:*
1 Top stands in front of the bottom partner who assumes a lunge position
2 The bottom partner, taking hold of top's hands, assists in a vertical step up onto one knee
3 Top slowly bends free leg, lifting it past and over the bottom partner's shoulder
4 Once the balance is stable, bottom partner transfers hand support to position shown

### Variations

An attitude scale (figure 64)
A 'Y' scale (figure 65)

### Thighstand star balance (figures 66 and 67)

*Points to note:*
1 The bottom partner forms a firm base by placing feet apart and bending knees to a squat stand

2 Taking hold of top's hands, he confidently assists top to a standing position on thighs
3 Top lifts right leg and places foot behind his partner's neck
4 Slowly releasing top's right hand, the bottom partner raises his left arm to produce a vice-like grip round top's foot
5 Ensuring that the balance is stable, he releases the other hand and top stretches arms above head into a star-shaped balance
6 The bottom partner can maintain control by leaning backwards to counterbalance the weight

### Hand-to-foot balance

Confidence in oneself and one's partner is a must in any acrobatic exercise and progress will be made in direct ratio to the trust developing between the partners.

It is imperative to understand the hand-to-foot range of movement, i.e. when the lower

Figure 63

Figure 64

Figure 65

Figure 66

Figure 67

partner supports the balance by holding the upper partner's foot or feet. Study closely the grip and the exercise progressions depicted in the illustrations (figures 68, 69, 70 and 71).

Repetition of these exercises will give the partners a sound understanding of timing which will result in a positive awareness of each other.

  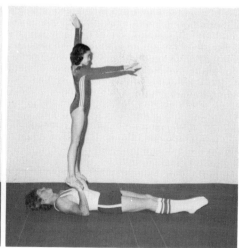

Figure 68

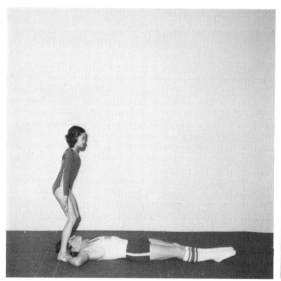 

Figure 70

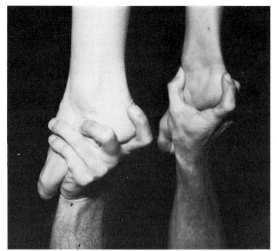

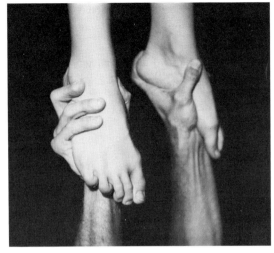

Figure 69

*Points to note:*

1 First become familiar with the balance (figure 68)

2 Both partners should concentrate on keeping the foot at an angle of 45° (figure 69)

3 The top partner must tighten stomach muscles and stretch body upwards at all times

4 The top partner stands with feet in bottom partner's hands, bends legs and, with a forward lift of the arms, jumps vertically to an extended stretch position. The bottom partner will have no problem maintaining the balance if top remains stretched with arms above head (figure 70)

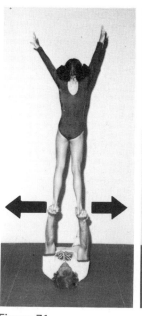

Figure 71

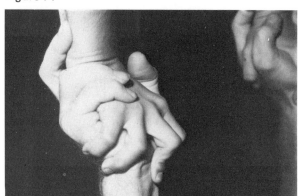

Figure 72

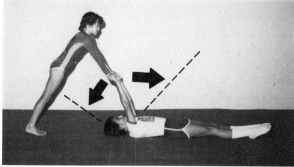

Figure 74

Figure 73

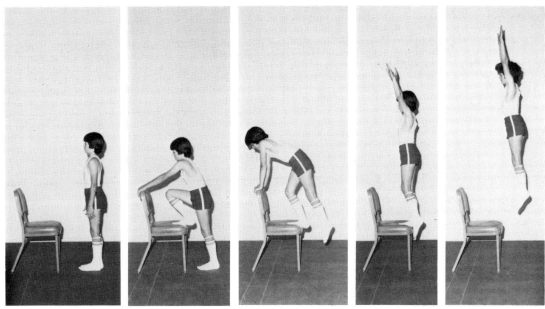

Figure 75

5 The bottom partner should vary the balance by moving top's feet apart, together, in small circles, and by balancing one foot at a time (figure 71)

## Hand-to-hand balance

In a hand-to-hand balance, each finger has a role to play. The correct use of finger position is essential (figure 72). The best hand-balancer in the world would have difficulty in maintaining a controlled balance if the lower partner provides an unstable base. In order to achieve a proper hand-to-hand balance (figure 73) you must go through the following steps.

1 The lower partner lies on his back and top stands at his head facing his feet
2 The partners take hands and form a comfortable grip
3 Both partners must be aware of what it feels like to go into an off-balance position and be confident that they are able to correct this (figure 74). This is where the correct use of finger position is essential (figure 72)

## The pitch

The pitch or throw involves the lower partner assisting the upper partner to achieve flight. It is essential for the upper partner to achieve a proper take-off and this must be practised many times. A chair or strong box placed against a wall will provide a platform, as shown in figure 75, and will help you understand what degree and angle of thrust are required from the bent leg. Make a positive effort to look over the back of the chair or apparatus, thus maintaining the body's centre of gravity over the take-off platform. When performing the pitch this is essential to enable the bottom partner to achieve a vertical lift.

The lower partner must also practise his part (figure 76) – knees together, back straight.

Make a habit of always preparing correctly. Stand facing each other. Top takes one or two controlled steps forward while the bottom partner moves into the squat position. Make the move as smooth as possible and avoid stops and jerks (figure 77).

### Shoulder/knee balance, sitting (figure 78)

*Points to note:*

1 Bottom partner sits with legs straddled. Top stands between bottom's legs with hands on his shoulders
2 Bottom partner, firmly holding top's thighs just above the knees and assisted by a jump from top, lifts his partner above his head to a tuck position
3 Top must take some of the weight by keeping arms straight and shoulders forward of hands
4 A spotter should always be there to guide the top partner to the correct balance position
5 The bottom partner must keep his head up and arms as straight as possible and must not round his back or the balance will be lost
6 Once this stage has been confidently reached, top can straighten one leg into a stag balance. Bottom partner may support the bent knee with both hands to start with. As the balance is secured, one hand may be released and extended to the side (figure 79)

Figure 76

Figure 77

Figure 78

## Shoulder stands (figure 80)

*Points to note:*

1 Bottom partner ensures a firm base by sitting on heels with legs slightly apart
2 Top, with his partner's assistance, steps up vertically onto his shoulders, providing an upward lift by extending arms above head
3 Top must press heels firmly together behind his partner's head
4 The bottom partner should hold top behind the calves and press his head firmly into top's shins in order to form a vice-like grip

### Variations

Attitude balance (figure 81)
'Y' scale balance (figure 82)

Always have spotters standing by when first attempting these skills.

Figure 79          Figure 80

## Climb to shoulder stand (figure 83)

The bottom partner makes a lunge to the side and the upper partner, stepping from behind, places his right foot on the bottom partner's right thigh and his left foot on his left shoulder. Continuing the smooth rhythm he moves his right foot onto the right shoulder. Balance is maintained by the partners holding hands. The top partner then stands up confidently – heels together and pressed down (figure 84), eyes focused forward – and raises hands above head. The bottom partner must lunge deep enough for a safe climb and he must remember to push his arms straight above as his partner is climbing.

Figure 83

Figure 81

Figure 82

Figure 84

### *Jump to shoulder stand* (figure 85)

The lower partner lunges forward, bending his rear leg sufficiently to form a take-off platform. Bending his arms back over his shoulders, he grasps top's hands, keeping elbows forward, shoulder-width apart. The top partner then places his foot on the lower partner's calf and, with the combined effort of top's jump and the thrust from the bent leg, the jump to shoulders will be achieved.

The lower partner should call the timing ('Ready – up'). The top partner must remember not to lean back but simply jump vertically, allowing his partner to absorb the shock of the jump.

### *Variations of feet-to-shoulder balances* (figures 86, 87, 88 and 89), front scale and 'Y' scale

*Points to note:*

1 Bottom partner must maintain a firm base position with feet astride
2 Top must move into the scale position slowly and positively
3 Top must avoid moving supporting foot on partner's shoulder. The heel should be kept down and balance maintained on the entire sole of the supporting foot
4 Bottom partner should ensure a firm grip on top's leg by wrapping his hand around the upper part of top's calf. He must press his head against top's shin to form a vice-like hold on his partner
5 Always have spotters standing by when first attempting this balance

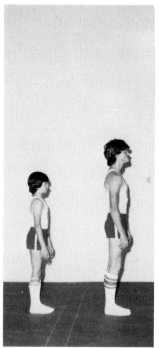

Figure 85

Figure 87

Figure 86

Figure 88

Figure 89

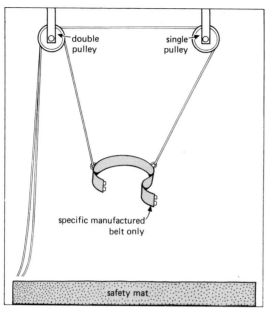

Figure 90

## Spotting belt (figure 90)

This is an extremely useful piece of equipment for coach and gymnast alike. It should be erected in a convenient and safe place. Ensure that the section of the roof to which the pulleys and clamps are to be attached is safe and strong enough to hold the stress that will be applied. It is advisable to seek professional assistance in the fitting of such equipment.

# 5 Dance

Dance is an essential, though often ignored, element in sports acrobatics. It can be defined as those movements that link the individual elements together and give a routine its continuity, flow and beauty.

With the addition of music and dance, a simple series of balances and skills can be transformed into a competitive routine.

Even if every pair or group performs the same acrobatic skills, the use of music and dance gives them the chance to express themselves individually. Each pair becomes unique and the gymnasts have the opportunity to convey their personalities to the audience.

The selection of music is very important. It determines the tempo and the mood of the routine and must also, of course, fulfil the requirements laid down for competition. For instance, the routine and therefore the music must not exceed two and a half minutes and there must be no lyrics.

To start with, use your own and your students' knowledge of dance to compose the dance portion of the routines. The opportunity for imaginative use of movement and variation of simple dance steps is boundless and gymnasts often create the most interesting and effective routines for themselves. As the skill and level of competition progresses, it will probably be necessary to enlist the aid of a choreographer.

## Some fundamental dance movements

*The march* (figure 91): as in an ordinary walk, the legs and arms move in opposition to each other. Greater opposition can be accomplished by exaggerating the arm and leg movements. For example, when leading with the right foot, extend the left arm forward with the right arm extended sideways parallel to the floor. Different arm positions add variety and interest to the basic

Figure 91

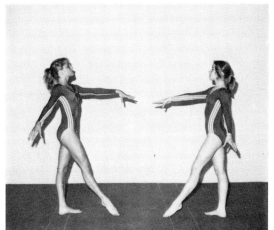

Figure 92

march. Many variations can be created by an imaginative coach or gymnast.

*The kick* (figure 92): simple but effective, the kick is an often used, very basic dance element in sports acrobatics routines. Make

Figure 93

sure the toes are pointed on the kick. Proper positioning of the hands and head is equally important in making the kick look polished and impressive.

*The split leap* (figure 93): a basic split leap consists of jumping forward, leading and landing on the same foot. Opposition can be added by kicking the back foot up or by extending an arm sideways. The standard split leap can be varied in countless ways: for example bend front knee (stag leap), bend back leg to touch head (arched jeté leap), bend both legs (double leg stag), switch legs in mid-air (double splits).

*Turning*: turning is almost limitless in variation and is a very important dance element to include in a sports acrobatics routine as it enables the gymnast to change direction. Without turns, routines would

Figure 94

Figure 95

consist entirely of linear movements and would consequently be much less interesting to perform and to watch.

The half turn and the full turn are the most commonly used. To initiate the movement, the arms (in opposition), head and torso twist in the desired direction of the spin. The body must be tense, and, in order to keep balance, the gymnast should use the ballet dancer's technique. The eyes should be fixed on one spot for as long as possible while the body turns and the head snapped round quickly to follow at the last moment (eyes refocusing on the same spot in the case of a full turn).

## Some basic poses

Poses are the static positions performed most often before or after a balance or tumbling portion of the routine. They give the gymnast time either to concentrate on the next move or to rest after a difficult move has just been completed. Some basic poses from which others can be developed are as follows:

*The lunge* (figure 94): bend the front leg, keeping the back leg straight and torso erect. The arms can be in any position – use your imagination.

*The scale* (figure 95): stand on one leg. The other leg must be kept straight and can be stretched behind, in front or to the side of the body. Remember to point your toes.

*Knee stand* (figure 96): balance on the mat on one knee. Place one arm overhead and the other sideways. Use your imagination to vary arm positions.

*Splits* (figure 97): legs are placed in opposition to each other. Variety can be added by body and arm positions.

Figure 96

Figure 97

# 6 Junior Competitive Programme

This chapter outlines a competitive programme for the novice. The events, their contents and the rules by which they are judged precede the suggested routines.

You will note that there are two events in this competitive programme that are not mentioned in any of the previous chapters – girls' trio and men's fours. Both trio and fours work is an extension of pair work and gymnasts must master the novice pair exercises before proceeding with group work. Essentially pair work is the foundation for all group exercises and if the progressions are overlooked, then logical, safe learning patterns will be impeded.

There are seven events in the competitive sports acrobatics programme:

Men's tumbling
Women's tumbling
Women's pairs
Men's pairs
Mixed pairs
Women's trio
Men's fours

The first two of these are individual events and the remaining five are group events. The individual gymnast need only compete in one event but may choose to compete in others so long as he does not compete in the same event twice.

## Tumbling (boys and girls)

Non-stop combinations of flips, springs, turns, etc., performed in a dynamic straight line. An approach run precedes and a stationary stand follows the tumbling skills.

## Group events

All group events are performed in the style of an artistic gymnastics floor exercise and a routine must display the following:

Balance: handstands, headstands, footstands
Tempo: flight elements, i.e. somersaults, springs, etc.
Individual elements: balance, flexibility, strength, tumbling, choreography

## Judging criteria

All group events are scored in a manner similar to that of artistic gymnastics, diving and figure skating. A maximum point score is based on the content, form and execution of the routine. Deductions are made in accordance with faults and deviations from the prescribed performance.

Tumbling is also judged in this way, except that synchronization, choreography and music are not factors.

A team score is arrived at by adding the top three scores in each event.

## Competitive rules

All competitors begin with a score of 10.00. The value of each element is indicated next to that element. Elements may be changed in part (left cartwheel to right, for example) so long as it does not affect the composition of the routine. All elements must be performed in the order shown. Balance elements are held for 2 seconds (not applicable to tumbling). Tempo elements should be performed with amplitude, rhythm and synchronization when indicated in the group events.

## Deductions

For group events and tumbling:

1 If an element is omitted the full value of that element is deducted
2 If the balance is not held for 2 seconds, 0.2–0.5 marks are deducted
3 Small break in form, e.g. legs not straight, toes not pointed, arms slightly bent, 0.1–0.2
4 Small lack of amplitude or rhythm, 0.1–0.2
5 Small step or steps on landing, 0.1–0.2
6 Major break in form and execution, 0.3–0.5
7 Major break in amplitude or rhythm, 0.3–0.5
8 Large steps or fall on landing, 0.3–0.5
9 General impression, including visible effort, untidy appearance, insufficient lightness, poor presentation, 0.1–0.5

For group events only:

10 Small lack of synchronization between partners, 0.1–0.2
11 Major lack of synchronization between partners, 0.3–0.5

For tumbling events only:

12 Loss of momentum, up to 0.5
13 Stops or additional steps between elements, routine is considered to have terminated at that point
14 Loss of direction causing gymnast to leave the mat, routine is considered to have terminated at that point

## Junior level competitive routines

*Tumbling sets (boys and girls)*

First routine

| 1 forward roll (tuck) | 1.0 |
|---|---|
| high jump | 0.5 |
| forward roll (tuck) | 1.0 |
| star jump | 0.5 |
| forward roll (tuck) | 1.0 |
| jump with 360° turn | 1.0 |
| | 5.0 |

| 2 handstand forward roll | 1.5 |
|---|---|
| high jump | 0.5 |
| forward roll walkout | 1.0 |
| handstand forward roll | 1.5 |
| high jump | 0.5 |
| | 5.0 |

Second routine

| 1 cartwheel | 1.0 |
|---|---|
| chassé | 0.5 |
| cartwheel | 1.0 |
| chassé | 0.5 |
| round-off | 2.0 |
| | 5.0 |

| 2 round-off jump half turn | 1.5 |
|---|---|
| cartwheel | 1.0 |
| chassé | 0.5 |
| cartwheel | 1.0 |
| round-off | 1.0 |
| | 5.0 |

Third routine

| 1 front handspring walkout | 2.0 |
|---|---|
| cartwheel | 1.0 |
| front handspring | 2.0 |
| | 5.0 |

| 2 round-off back handspring | 2.0 |
|---|---|
| jump turn walkout cartwheel | 1.0 |
| round-off back handspring | 2.0 |
| | 5.0 |

## Women's pairs

First routine (figure 98)
Starting position: partners face each other, seven to eight paces apart

1 Both partners forward roll, step onto one leg and move into a front scale position holding hands (hold for 2 seconds). Lower legs to standing position      2.5

2 Top partner climbs onto lower partner's thighs and extends backwards (hold for 2 seconds)      2.0

3 Both partners extend right arms to side in synchronization. Return to original position and repeat to the left (hold for 2 seconds each time)      1.5

4 Top jumps to floor      1.5

5 Both partners half turn (180°), immediately cartwheel and complete the routine by standing, legs together, in the finishing position      2.5

         10.00

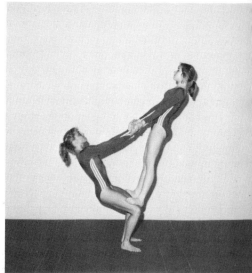

Figure 98

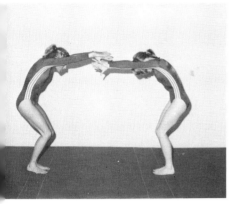

Second routine (figure 99)
Starting position: partners face each other, two to three paces apart

1  Lower partner backward rolls to a stag split position, arms reaching forward at a 45° angle ............... 1.0
2  Simultaneously, top partner forward rolls to a front scale position. Partners clasp hands (hold for 2 seconds) ............... 1.0
3  Lower partner rises up onto knees while top half turns with arms vertical ............... 1.0
4  Lower partner extends backwards and grasps ankles. Top backbends to place hands on partner's waist (hold for 2 seconds) ............... 1.0
5  Top returns to stand and partner rises up on one knee. Top takes hold of partner's hands and steps up backwards to stand on the knee. Hold an attitude position with free leg (hold for 2 seconds) ............... 2.5
6  Top steps down and half turns to face partner ............... 0.5
7  Top kicks to a stag handstand. Partner supports foot ............... 1.5
8  Lower partner extends backwards and places free hand on the floor ............... 1.0
9  Both partners return to standing position for finish ............... 0.5

10.00

Figure 99

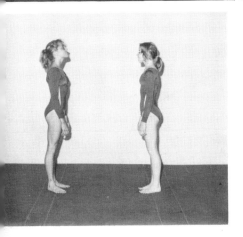

Third routine (figure 100)
Starting position: top stands behind partner, one pace away

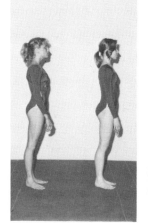

| | |
|---|---|
| 1 Both partners backbend. Lower partner places hands on top's thighs (hold for 2 seconds) | 1.5 |
| 2 Both return to standing | 1.0 |
| 3 Lower partner lies on back with knees bent. Top places hands on partner's knees and moves into horizontal front support, secured by lower partner holding top's knees (hold for 2 seconds) | 1.0 |
| 4 Top bends one knee and holds for 2 seconds | 0.5 |
| 5 Lower partner sits up and straightens legs, at the same time assisting top to a stag handstand, supporting this by holding the bent knee | 2.0 |
| 6 Top lowers bent leg to partner's side and stands | 0.5 |
| 7 Lower partner slides to a lying position with legs straight at an angle of 45°. Top, raising arms over head, extends to a back swan position, supported at the hands (hold for 2 seconds) | 1.5 |
| 8 Top raises one knee to a stag position and, at the same time, releases hands to the side (hold for 2 seconds) | 1.0 |
| 9 Top steps down forwards, both cartwheel and finish in standing position | 1.0 |
| | 10.00 |

Figure 100

## Men's pairs

First routine (figure 101)
Starting position: partners face each other

| | |
|---|---|
| 1 Both partners lunge | 0.5 |
| 2 Top kicks to handstand, supported by partner at legs | 2.0 |
| 3 Top returns to standing and climbs on partner's thighs, holding hands for support | 2.0 |
| 4 Lower partner transfers his grip from top's hands to thighs | 2.0 |
| 5 Top jumps down with tuck, partner assisting | 2.0 |
| 6 Both cartwheel and finish in standing position | 1.5 |
| | 10.00 |

Second routine (figure 102)
Starting position: partners face each other, one pace apart

| | |
|---|---|
| 1 Top kicks to an assisted handstand | 1.0 |
| 2 Top lowers onto his shoulders as though going into a roll. His partner grasps his ankles and with a strong pull and push action, assisted by the thrust from top's arms, directs him through a back flip to a standing position | 2.5 |
| 3 Top performs a forward roll while his partner straddle leaps over him. Both then leap with twist | 2.0 |
| 4 Partners perform a pitch, lower partner assisting the landing by holding partner's hands | 2.5 |
| 5 Top springs upwards with a half turn | 1.0 |
| 6 Both partners arch leap with a 90° turn | 0.5 |
| 7 Both partners forward roll and finish in a standing position | 0.5 |
| | 10.00 |

Figure 101

Figure 102

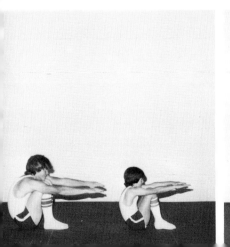

Third routine (figure 103)
Starting position: partners face each other

| | |
|---|---:|
| 1 Top leaps to stand on partner's knees | 0.5 |
| 2 Lower partner sits then lies, top partner all the while maintaining contact at hands and knees | 2.0 |
| 3 Top tuck jumps through partner's arms to dismount and half turns | 1.0 |
| 4 With the support of lower partner's upraised legs, top stands on his partner's hands for a low hand to foot stand | 2.0 |
| 5 Top jumps to tuck position on partner's straight legs, dismounts forwards and half turns | 0.5 |
| 6 Partners perform a shoulder/knee balance | 2.0 |
| 7 Top dismounts by continuing into a forward walkover and half turns | 1.5 |
| 8 Top assists partner to standing position finish by pulling up with hands | 0.5 |
| | 10.00 |

Figure 103

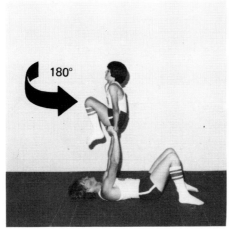

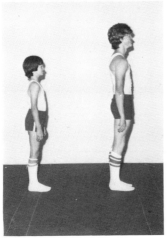

## Mixed pairs

First routine (figure 104)
Starting position: partners face each other, one pace apart

1 Top takes hold of partner's hands and steps up onto thighs, and, maintaining contact at hands, extends backwards ......... 0.5
2 Bottom partner, using top to counterbalance the weight, lowers through sitting to prone position with top balanced on hands and knees ......... 2.5
3 Top dismounts by stepping forward through arms to the floor ......... 1.5
4 Top backbends to take partner's hands – he supports top on bent arms ......... 1.5
5 Top returns to standing assisted by a controlled push ......... 0.5
6 Top half turns ......... 0.5
7 Top takes hold of partner's hands and jumps through arms to stand on knees ......... 1.5
8 Lower partner, using top to counterbalance weight, rises through sitting to standing position. Balance is held for 2 seconds. Top jumps down and both finish in standing position. ......... 1.5

10.00

Figure 104

Second routine (figure 105)
Starting position: partners face each other, five to six paces apart

1 Both partners forward roll, the lower partner finishing in a lying position, legs bent at the knee  1.0
2 Top places hands on partner's knees and pushes into a shoulder/knee balance  1.5
3 Top lowers to floor and assists partner to feet  1.5
4 Lower partner steps into forward lunge and, taking top's hands, assists her to step up onto his shoulders using thigh and shoulder as a ladder  2.0
5 Both partners simultaneously move their arms to the side and display free balance for 2 seconds  2.0
6 Top takes hold of partner's hands and with his assistance tuck jumps to floor and finishing position  2.0

10.00

Figure 105

Third routine (figure 106)
Starting position: partners face each other, two to three paces apart

1 Top steps into a pitch with supported landing                                          1.0
2 Lower partner forward lunges and top takes hold of his hands for support in a back extension stand    0.5
3 Top moves into front scale position and then lowers to sit with one leg extended to the front, all the while maintaining hand contact with her partner    1.0
4 With her partner's assistance, top jumps into a horizontal front lying position, supported under stomach and thighs    2.0
5 Lower partner tosses top up with a half turn to catch her in a horizontal back lying position    1.5
6 Top backbends to handstand supported by her partner in the lower back and continues to stag position supported at the foot of the straight leg    1.5
7 Top forward rolls out of the handstand with her partner still maintaining contact with her foot. Top only rolls to her back and her partner then takes hold of both ankles and with a strong pull and push action directs her through a back flip to a standing position, with assisted landing. Both partners finish in standing position    2.5

                                                                                    10.00

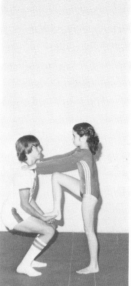

Figure 106

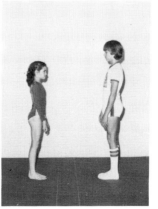

*Girls' trio*

First routine (figure 107)
Starting position: middle, bottom, top stand one behind each other in that order, one pace between each

| | |
|---|---|
| 1 All backward roll to one knee | 1.5 |
| 2 Middle steps into front scale position, holding bottom partner's hands. Top raises both arms above head and backbends to place hands on bottom partner's forward knee | 1.0 |
| 3 All stand and top half turns to face bottom partner. Bottom partner lies down with knees bent and top kicks to a shoulder/knee balance. Middle goes into a front lunge and supports top's foot in a stag stand | 2.0 |
| 4 Top brings feet together, middle steps forward with half turn, raises hands above head and backbends to place hands on top's back | 2.5 |
| 5 Middle returns to standing and half turns to face the other two. Top brings legs straight down to the floor and drops to one knee. Middle takes hold of bottom partner's hands and jumps through arms to stand on knees | 1.5 |
| 6 Bottom partner rises up to standing, using middle to counterbalance weight. Top remains kneeling. Middle lifts one leg up to 45° angle and top supports by the foot | 1.0 |
| 7 Top stands with half turn, middle steps down and all three finish in standing position facing forward | 0.5 |
| | 10.00 |

Figure 107

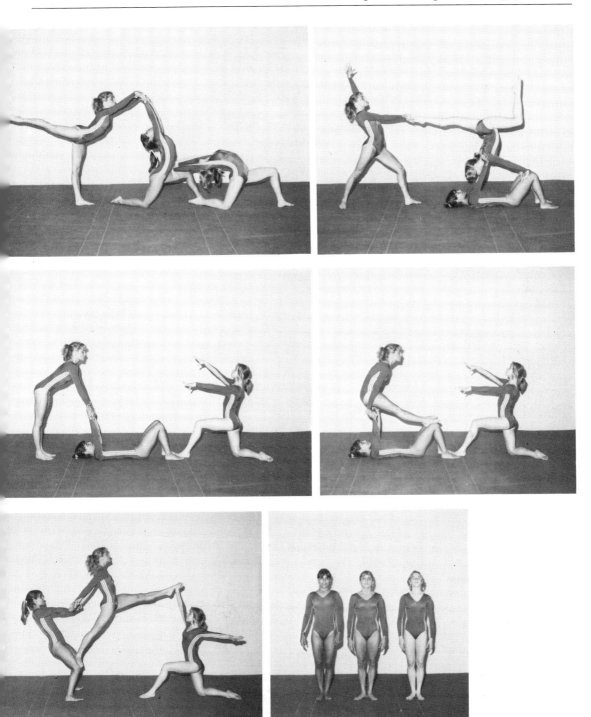

Second routine (figure 108)
Starting position: bottom, top, middle stand one behind the other, one pace between each. Middle half turns to face top

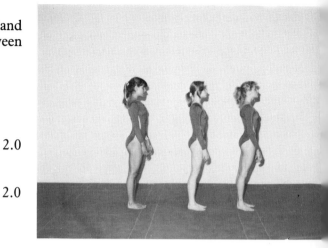

1 Top jumps back onto bottom partner's thighs. Bottom partner transfers support from waist to thighs, and middle, showing forward lunge, holds top's hands    2.0

2 Middle releases top's hands and kicks to handstand, supported by top (hold for 2 seconds)    2.0

3 Middle returns to standing, takes hold of top's hands and assists with a high jump to the floor. Top immediately slides into forward splits    1.0

4 Bottom and middle partners step to the side and, facing top, move into front scale position, holding top's hands    2.0

5 Middle half turns and, together with bottom partner, lowers to a squat. Top moves into sitting position with knees bent    0.5

6 All roll backwards to shoulder balance with legs vertical    1.0

7 All bend one leg    0.5

8 All place legs together, forward roll to stand, jump and half turn into finish position    1.0

       10.00

Figure 108

Third routine (figure 109)
Starting position: bottom and middle partners on one knee facing each other, top standing between to form triangle

1 Top takes hold of both partners' hands and moves into front scale while they show backward extension      1.0
2 Bottom and middle partners grasp free hands together and top jumps over them      1.0
3 Top backward rolls to original position, while the other two raise their hands above their heads      1.0
4 Top places one hand on each partners' knee and, assisted by them, kicks to handstand supported at the waist      2.0
5 Top moves legs to straddle position and the other two release one hand      2.0
6 Top returns to standing and raises arms to sides. The other two turn and kick to handstand supported by top      2.0
7 Bottom and middle partners return to standing and all three move into finishing position      1.0

                                             10.00

Figure 109

## Men's fours

### First routine (figure 110)

1 Bottom partner lies on his back, legs raised. First middle, with legs bent, is supported in lower back by bottom partner's feet, in a chair shape. Second middle moves into a shoulder/knee balance with bottom partner. Top kicks to handstand on knees of first middle with assistance at hips. Hold balance for 3 seconds. All return to standing     5.0

2 Bottom partner lies on his back and supports top in a shoulder/knee balance. First middle, in a chair position, supports second middle in a thigh stand on his hips. Second middle assists top with balance. Hold balance for 3 seconds. All return to standing     5.0

                          10.00

Figure 110

### Second routine (figure 111)
Starting position: top and second middle partners stand behind first middle and bottom partners respectively

1 Simultaneously both pairs grasp hands overhead and first middle and bottom partners step into forward lunge. Top and second middle step up via backs of partners' legs to stand on their shoulders. The lower two partners support the upper two at the calves     4.0

2 Both pairs grasp hands and move into tuck balances. Hold for 3 seconds     4.0

3 The upper two partners jump down forwards to land in front of the lower two in finishing position     2.0

                          10.00

Figure 111

**Third routine (figure 112)**
Starting position: the two middle partners assume chair positions side by side, bottom partner standing behind with top in front

1 Middle partners pitch top upwards at an angle over their heads to land assisted by bottom partner     4.0
2 Middle partners turn to face each other and form a basket by clasping hands. Top leaps backwards onto basket while bottom moves to the front of middle partners     1.0
3 Middle partners toss top into back flip assisted by bottom partner     3.0
4 Bottom assists top in landing and all show finish position     2.0

——————
10.00

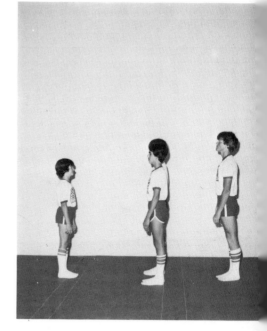

## Goals of the junior competitive programme

The major goal of coaches and judges should be to promote safe, well-executed and entertaining performances. If the judges reward risk and difficulty at the expense of execution, they are doing a grave injustice to the sport, its coaches, and, of course, the gymnasts themselves. Don't be satisfied with a shoddy routine. Use form throughout. Resist the temptation to skip to the next skill or balance before the present one has been mastered. All junior competitors should consistently achieve a score of 8.00 in the compulsory exercises before attempting to compose their own optional routines.

Schools, universities, colleges and clubs are encouraged to use this junior programme to stage internal or inter-club competitions in order to bring novices to the point where they can begin to create their own routines, with the introduction of the music and choreography which is necessary for senior level competition.

Figure 112